D1581877

The History of the Camera

Elizabeth Raum

www.heinemann.co.uk/library
Visit our website to find out more information about Heinemann Library books.

To order:
 Phone 44 (0)1865 888066
 Send a fax to 44 (0)1865 314091
 Visit the Heinemann Bookshop at www.heinemann.co.uk/library to browse our catalogue and order online.

First published in Great Britain by Heinemann Library, Halley Court, Jordan Hill, Oxford OX2 8EJ, part of Harcourt Education.
Heinemann is a registered trademark of Harcourt Education Ltd.

Editorial: Kristen Truhlar and Diyan Leake
Design: Victoria Bevan and Tower Designs Ltd
Picture research: Mica Brancic
Production: Julie Carter

Origination: Dot Gradations
Printed and bound in China by South China Printing Co. Ltd

ISBN 978 0 431 19146 1
12 11 10 09 08
10 9 8 7 6 5 4 3 2 1

British Library Cataloguing in Publication Data
Raum, Elizabeth
The history of the camera. - (Inventions that changed the world)
1. Cameras - History - Juvenile literature 2. Photography - History - Juvenile literature 3. Photography - Social aspects - Juvenile literature
I. Title
303.4'83
ISBN-13: 9780431191461

Acknowledgements
The publishers would like to thank the following for permission to reproduce photographs: p. **4** Getty Images/Robert Harding World Imagery, p. **5** Corbis/The State Russian Museum, p. **6** Science & Society Picture Library/Science Museum, p. **7** Science & Society Picture Library/NMPFT, p. **8** Corbis/Michael Freeman, p. **9** The Art Archive/Culver Pictures, p. **10** Topham Picturepoint, p. **11** Science & Society Picture Library/National Museum of Photography, p. **12** akg-images, p. **13** Corbis/Bettman, p. **14** Topham Picturepoint, p. **15** Science Photo Library/Library of Congress, p. **16** Topham Picturepoint, p. **17** Advertising Archives, p. **18** Science & Society Picture Library/National Museum of Photography, p. **19** Corbis/H. Armstrong Roberts, p. **20** Science & Society Picture Library/National Museum of Photography, p. **21** Advertising Archives, p. **22** Science Photo Library/Planetary Visions Ltd, p. **23** Getty Images/Photographer's Choice (Alamy), p. **24** akg-images, p. **25** Science Photo Library/Cordelia Molloy, p. **26** Masterfile/Michael Goldman (Getty/Photodisc), p. **27** Photolibrary.com/Pacific Stock/Carl Roessler (Alamy/Paul Springett).

Cover photograph of a camera from around 1900, reproduced with permission of Corbis/Hulton Deutsch Collection.

Contents

Before cameras 4

The first camera 6

Daguerre makes better photos. 8

Talbot's photos on paper. 10

Using cameras 12

George Eastman's idea 14

Cameras for everyone 16

Flash and colour. 18

Instant pictures 20

Digital cameras. 22

Cameras that help people. 24

How cameras changed life 26

Timeline. 28

World map activity. .29

Find out more. 30

Glossary 31

Index. 32

Some words are shown in bold, **like this**. You can find out what they mean by looking in the glossary.

Before cameras

People everywhere enjoy looking at pictures. From the earliest days, people have drawn pictures. Pictures help us remember places, people, and events.

People drew this picture in a cave in France thousands of years ago.

Painting a picture like this one sometimes took weeks or months.

Before there were cameras, artists painted pictures. Many of the paintings were beautiful, but they took a long time to finish. Sometimes the paintings did not look real.

The first camera

For many years, people wanted to make a camera. The **camera obscura** came first. It made a picture, but the picture had to be copied by hand onto paper.

This machine, called a camera obscura, was a very early kind of camera.

This is Joseph Niépce's first photo. It was fuzzy, but it was a start.

A man in France called Joseph Niépce had a new idea. He used **chemicals** to make a picture on a piece of **metal**. In 1826 he took a **photograph** (also called photo) of the buildings and fields outside his window. He had **invented** the camera.

Daguerre makes better photos

Louis Daguerre, who was also from France, worked with Niépce. In 1839 Daguerre found a way to make the photos taken on Niépce's camera last a long time. He called his photos **daguerreotypes**.

Louis Daguerre's first camera looked like a wooden box.

Most early daguerreotype photos like this one were of people.

Newspaper writers wrote stories about Daguerre's new way of making photos. People wanted to learn more. Daguerre wrote a book explaining how to make daguerreotypes. The book was printed in eight languages.

Talbot's photos on paper

Louis Daguerre's photos were printed on **metal**. In 1839 William Henry Fox Talbot, an **inventor** from England, found a way to print photos on paper. We still print photos on paper today.

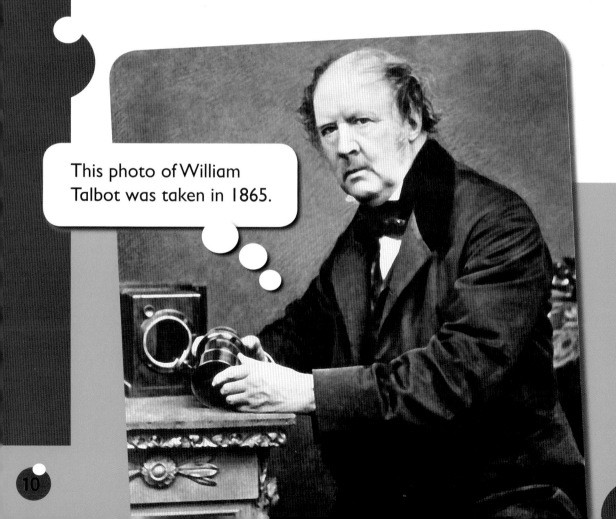

This photo of William Talbot was taken in 1865.

Talbot's first photo was called *The Handshake*.

Talbot learned how to make more than one copy of a **photograph**. He printed a book of nature pictures in 1844. It was the first book with photographs.

Using cameras

In the middle of the 1800s, **photography studios** opened all over Europe and the United States. Children and entire families **posed** for photos. People sent the photos to friends. They kept the photos to look at in later years.

These children posed for a photo in a photography studio.

A photographer took this school photo in 1885.

Photographers began taking cameras out into the world. They travelled to places most people could not go. These pictures helped people learn what was happening around the world.

George Eastman's idea

Many of the first cameras were very big and hard to carry. These cameras used heavy **plates** instead of **film**. **Inventors** around the world tried to make cameras that were smaller and easier to use.

This huge camera was used to take a photo of a train.

People taking photos needed a big camera, a stand to hold the camera, and heavy plates. George Eastman, of the United States, wanted to find an easier way to take photos. In 1884 he **invented** film on a roll.

George Eastman mad it easier for people to take photos.

Cameras for everyone

George Eastman began a company called Kodak. In 1888 the first Kodak camera was sold. It was smaller than earlier cameras. Many people bought the first Kodak camera even though it cost a lot of money.

The first Kodak camera came with its own case.

Brownie cameras were sold around the world.

In 1900 Kodak **invented** a camera called the Brownie. Kodak's Brownie camera was easy to use. Millions of children and adults bought Brownie cameras. Kodak sold Brownies for 70 years.

Flash and colour

Cameras got better over time. A man from Germany called Oskar Barnack **invented** a new kind of camera. He called it a Leica. It was the first **35 millimetre camera**. In 1924 people started buying Leica cameras.

By the 1930s, cameras came in many shapes and sizes.

This news photographer is
using a camera with a big f

In 1930 the flash camera was invented.
The flash of light let **photographers** take
photos in dark places. By 1936 a new kind
of **film** made colour photos possible. More
people bought colour film than black
and white.

Instant pictures

In 1944 a man in the United States named Edwin Land took a photo of his three-year-old daughter. She asked to see the photo right away. That gave him an idea.

The first Polaroid cameras folded up when not in use.

In 1947 Land **invented** an **instant** camera. It was called a Polaroid. Minutes after the picture was snapped, a photo came out of the camera.

Digital cameras

In the 1970s, **astronauts** wanted to take photos in space and send them back to Earth quickly. **Inventors** made the digital camera. Digital cameras do not need **film**. The photos are stored on a tiny computer disk inside the camera.

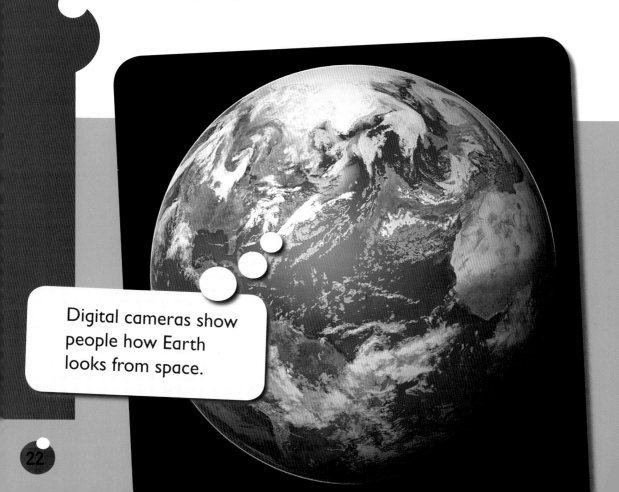

Digital cameras show people how Earth looks from space.

Today many mobile phones can take photos.

It took time to make the digital camera smaller and easy to use. In 1991 Kodak began selling digital cameras to the public. In 2000 a company in Japan put a camera in a mobile phone. Now many companies make camera phones.

Cameras that help people

Today we can use cameras to help keep us safe. Cameras help guard banks from robbers. Cameras in schools help guard students from strangers. Cameras watch busy roads so that the police know when there are problems.

This camera takes photos of everyone who passes by it.

Doctors also use cameras. Doctors use X-ray cameras to see broken bones. In 2005 an **inventor** put a camera in a pill. It lets doctors see inside a person's body.

A pill camera is very tiny.

How cameras changed life

Before cameras, people had to draw or paint pictures. Now cameras make it easy to have photos every day. Cameras also make it easy to remember the past. We can look at old photos to learn about life long ago.

Today it is easy to take photos.

This **photographer** is taking pictures under water with a special camera.

Cameras take us to places we cannot go. They take us into space or under water. In the future, cameras will take even better photos. They will be even easier to use.

Timeline

1826 Joseph Niépce **invents** the camera.

1839 Louis Daguerre invents **daguerreotypes**.

1839 William Talbot prints photos on paper.

1884 George Eastman invents **film** on a roll.

1888 Kodak camera is for sale.

1924 Oskar Barnack's **35 millimetre camera** is for sale.

1930 Flash camera is invented.

1935 Colour film is invented.

1947 Edwin Land invents the Polaroid **instant** camera.

1975 Digital camera is invented.

1991 Digital camera is for sale.

2000 Camera phone is invented.

2005 Pill camera is first used.

World map activity

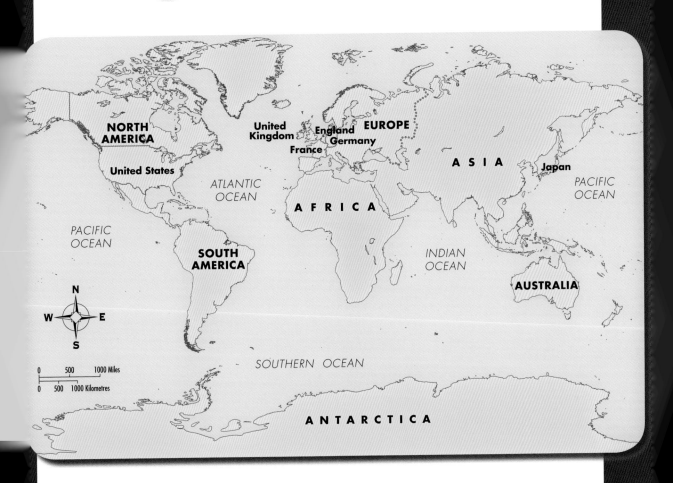

The countries talked about in this book are labelled on this world map. Try to find each **inventor**'s country on the map.

Find out more

Books

Breakthrough Inventions: Inventing the Camera, Joanne Richter (Crabtree, 2006).

Lives and Times: George Eastman, Jennifer Gillis (Heinemann Library, 2004).

Take Your Camera to... series, Ted Park (Raintree, 2003).

Websites

Enchanted Learning – http://www.enchantedlearning.com/inventors

Technology at Home – http://www.pbs.org/wgbh/aso/tryit/tech

Glossary

35 millimetre camera camera that uses special film that is 35 millimetres wide to take good pictures

astronaut someone who travels in space

camera obscura type of early camera that could not store photos

chemical substance mixed with other substances to make something happen

daguerreotype photo on metal

film roll of thin plastic used in a camera to store photos

instant happen right away

invent make something that did not exist before

inventor someone who makes something that did not exist before

metal hard, shiny material that melts when it is heated

photograph (photo) picture taken by a camera

photographer someone who uses a camera to take photos

photography studio room or building where pictures are taken

plate heavy piece of metal needed by early cameras to make a photo

pose stay still for a picture

Index

35 millimetre camera   18

Barnack, Oskar   18
Brownie camera   17

camera obscura   6
camera phone   23
chemicals   7
colour film   19

Daguerre, Louis   8-9, 10
daguerreotypes   8-9
digital camera   22-23

Eastman, George   15, 16
England   10
Europe   12film   14-15, 22

flash camera   19
France   7-8

Germany   18

Japan   23

Kodak   16-17, 23

Land, Edwin   20-21
Leica   18metal   7, 10

Niépce, Joseph   7-8

paintings   5
photographers   13, 19
photography studios   12
pill camera   25
plates   14-15
Polaroid camera   21

Talbot, William Henry Fox   10-11

United States, the   12, 20

X-ray camera   25